My Life as a Mayfly

My Life as a Mayfly

Rick Hafele

ISBN: 9798600882522

To:
Max, Meadow, Rocco, Emma & Claire

May the mystery always remain!

A Pale Morning Dun Speaks!

It's cold on the bottom of a trout stream. Of course, as a cold-blooded mayfly nymph adapted to cold trout streams, I find it rather comfortable. I'm sitting with a half dozen other nymphs on the bottom of a gentle riffle among golf ball to baseball size stones lazily grazing on diatoms and bits of algae like I've done every day for almost a year. I find it hard to keep track of time since every day is much like the one before, except that every day there seems to be fewer of us on the rocks grazing. I've also noticed lately that most of my brothers and sisters around me now have odd growths on their backs shaped like two dark brownish-black slippers. I can't see my own back, but it feels different and my skin seems to be getting tighter.

Suddenly a call goes out that an important meeting is scheduled and all the nymphs in my neighborhood must attend. Apparently the chief nymph has something critical to tell us. My buddies and I on the rock can hardly eat as this is the first time such a meeting has ever been called, and we have no idea what could be so important.

Hundreds - no thousands - of nymphs start moving towards a hollowed out area surrounded by waving aquatic plants. The afternoon sun reflects off the water, and the sky looks like spilled paint on the water's mirror-like surface. Crawling along the bottom may look safe, but moving from the rock

crevices to the meeting location is risky. If you loose your footing the current quickly takes you away, and we've been told from our first days as nymphs to stay out of the current at all costs - when you drift away you never come back!

Once gathered together around the aquatic plants we all settle into a comfortable resting place. Some hang on the leaves of the plants. Others sit in the sand at the base of the stems. I find a nice flat stone off to one side to crawl onto just as the chief nymph stands up on a piece of dead wood lodged in the stream bottom and begins explaining what is happening.

"Dear brothers and sisters this is the day you've all been eating for," he begins. "Within the next few days you will change in ways you can't imagine. You've all seen the dark slipper-like growths on everyone's back. And you've felt the tightness of your own skin. In the past such feelings meant you needed to find a safe place to hide while your tight outer skin fell off and new looser skin took its place. That was then, this is now."

The head nymph pauses waiting to make sure we are all paying close attention, then goes on. "The next time you feel the gentle warming of the water, when the late morning sun slowly raises the water temperature, you will have an uncontrollable urge to let go of the bottom and swim towards the surface."

"Yeah, right," I say to the nymph on my left. "That's the last thing I'm going to do. See those fish just above eyeing us? It would be suicide to leave the stream bottom."

The head nymph keeps talking, "You will try to resist, but resistance is futile and only prolongs the inevitable. It is the destiny of every nymph here and across the entire waterway to let go of the bottom and swim for the heavens above."

He now stands straight up on his two back legs using his tails for balance, "I repeat, every nymph here and across the entire waterway will let go of the stream bottom and head for the surface. Many of you won't make it. Some will be eaten just as you leave the cover of the bottom. Others will get swept up

in the swift currents and be carried downstream to waiting trout. Many of you, however, will make it, and for those the most amazing thing will happen." He now yells at the top of his gills, "Just before you reach the surface you will slip out of your tight skins, and instead of a new nymph skin underneath, you will find you have two pair of wings unfolding from your back. You will also notice that you are as mute as a clam, as you now have no mouth with which to speak, eat, or even drink a drop of water."

"Whoa, this is getting a little far out," I say as I look over at my buddy on the rock next to me. He looks back and quickly adds, "Why in the world would we all do something so dumb? I'm not going."

The head nymph continues, "You my be wondering, why would you do such a dangerous thing? Well, you may have heard stories that someday you will be able to fly through the air like birds. Of course you didn't believe these fairy tales, but I'm here to tell you now they are true. If you get to the surface and poke your body through the surface film, you will take off into the air like snowflakes rising up to the clouds." The head nymph's gills twitch up and down, "Then fly quickly to the nearest tree to hide and wait, for within another 24 hours you will molt your skin one last time."

His large eyes sparkle now as he prepares to finish his speech. "Once you've lost your last skin you will take to the air one last time to find your mate. The ladies will then lay their burden of eggs back onto the water's surface. Then all will sleep."

With that the head nymph drops down onto all six legs, walks slowly down the log, and disappears.

"That's the craziest thing I've ever heard," my buddy says, while flicking his tails up and down.

But just then he lets go of the stone he's on, and with a shocked look on his face he begins swimming up. When I look around dozens more, then hundreds more, then thousands more nymphs start swimming up. That's when I feel my own legs let go of the smooth round stone on the bottom and I'm floating downstream in the current.

"Holy nymph fest!" I yell as a nymph next to me disappears into a trout's mouth.

Other trout are swimming by with mouths open, darting left and right. Nymphs are disappearing left and right as well. I decide it is swim or get eaten, so swim I do. I swim like there's no tomorrow, and then suddenly my skin begins to split open. I'm still a foot or so below the surface.

"Just like the head nymph predicted," I yell, when suddenly I'm unable to speak.

Short crumpled wings poke out of my back, and I notice my body is no longer brown, but a beautiful pale yellow color. It is either by luck or grace that I make it to the surface, then through the surface. Others are there too, but not for long. It's crazy. From

above swallows dart down grabbing my kin off the water. From below trout keep coming up and sucking my buddies back down. I stretch my new wings until they feel stiff, then cross my tarsi hoping beyond hope to escape the attacks from above and below. I flap hard and suddenly, like magic, I feel freedom. I'm flying!

Once in the air swallows keep coming. One barely misses me but gets a similar looking brother right beside me.

As I head for the nearest tree I see a strange two-legged creature in the water

waving a long slender stem in the air. He seems to have one of my kind attached to a thread and is throwing it onto the water. It doesn't look much like me I think, but a trout sucks it down and he lets out a yell like some wild creature. I'm not going to complain if there is one less trout eating my buddies.

The next morning I again have the strangest feeling when suddenly my skin splits open, and within just a minute or two my pale yellow wings are as clear as glass and I feel lighter and quite excited.

The late morning air is mild and calm and I can see that many others of my kind also look different than yesterday, and have already started to fly off their leaves back into the sky. I think, "Well no sense in stopping now, lets go for it," and fly off with the others.

We now fill the sky twenty or thirty feet above the water. A swarm of millions, nearly all males, dance up and down in the sunlight. The swallows are back too, but to be honest I

don't care. I feel light as goose down as I flap my paper thin clear wings and dance up and down several feet through the air.

Thousands of us dance in unison and fill the sky. While flitting up and down I strain all the facets of my huge red eyes to find a pale rusty brown female any where in my vicinity.

There she is. A few feet above and just ahead of me. I give it all I have and fly up and wrap my long front legs around her thorax. We drop slowly towards the water while we hold each other in our one and only embrace.

Just before hitting the water she lets go and flies away. I never see her again. I start twirling in the breeze. I can see a swallow change directions and head my way. The swallow's mouth opens…….

Some Facts about Mayflies You Might not Know

Mayflies are a group of insects that live most of their life underwater. They are called nymphs during their underwater stage. There are many different kinds of mayflies. Some live in tiny streams, others in large rivers, and still others in lakes and ponds. In total more than 600 different species of mayflies live in waters across North America.

Mayflies are also ancient. Their ancestors lived over 300 million years ago. That's before the dinosaurs walked the earth, and they still live today.

Mayfly nymphs spend about a year underwater, eating aquatic plants and algae, and growing bigger. But in order to grow bigger every few weeks nymphs have to shed their outer skin, called the exoskeleton, so a new larger skin can take its place. This is called molting. Nymphs may molt 20-30 times as they grow underwater.

The dark black wingpads on the back of this mayfly nymph indicates that it is mature and will be ready to emerge into a winged mayfly soon.

Once the nymphs have finished growing they change in an amazing way. Fully grown nymphs swim up to the water's surface where their skin splits open as if to molt, but instead of molting into a larger nymph out pops a new body that has wings! Their new body also has two or three long tails, longer legs, and much larger eyes. This stage of the mayfly's life is called a dun. After resting a few seconds on the waters' surface to dry their wings the duns fly up into the air and try to reach the safety of shoreline vegetation.

A newly emerged mayfly dun rests on a leaf waiting to molt.

Mayfly duns can't eat because they don't have a mouth. They just sit quietly for about one or two days then molt, or shed their outer skin, one last time. After this molt they look different, and are now called a spinner. Their wings are now clear, their tails and legs are longer than the dun's, and the eyes of male spinners are huge. Mayfly spinners mate in the air, after which the females lay their eggs on the water's surface. After mating and laying eggs the spinners die, often on the water's surface.

A mayfly's whole life only lasts about one year, and they only live three or four days with wings. Because their winged stages live such a short time, entomologists have given mayflies the name Ephemeroptera, a Latin word that means *short-lived winged insect.*

Here is a male mayfly spinner with its clear wings and huge eyes.

Trout love to eat mayflies. In fact mayflies get eaten by a lot of different fish and animals. Besides trout what was eating Billy's brothers and sisters in this story?

Fly fishers also love mayflies. Not because they want to eat them, but because trout do. By tying artificial flies that look like mayflies, fly fishers can fool trout into eating one of their fake flies. If they can cast their fly onto the water so it looks like a real mayfly, then trout will eat it and the fly fisher will catch the trout. Sometimes fly fishers take the trout home to eat. but they can also release the trout back into the water alive.

This beautiful cutthroat trout got fooled by some fur and feathers tied on a hook to look like a mayfly!

Fly fishers have created hundreds of different looking flies to fool trout and other species of fish. Most flies are made out of different kinds of fur and feathers, but tinsel, wire, and metal or glass beads are also used to create a fly that looks like a mayfly or some different kind of food fish eat. Would you be fooled by one of these flies? It's a good thing trout aren't as smart as you!

The life of a mayfly is very different than yours. But even though mayflies live a very short life, they are very important to all the fish and birds that eat them. Without mayflies in our rivers and lakes there would be very few fish and not nearly as many birds singing by the rivers.

The next time you see a mayfly be sure to say THANK YOU!

Above: Just a few of the many different mayfly fly patterns used by fly fishers to catch trout.

ABOUT THE AUTHOR

Rick Hafele started fly fishing over 50 years ago and has worked as a professional aquatic biologist for over 40 years. For many years he has been sharing his knowledge of insects, streams and fish with fly fishers through books, articles, slide shows and DVDs. A list of other books he has authored and his instructional DVDs can be found on his website at: www.rickhafele.com

(Practice drawing and coloring the mayfly on the opposite page here.)

Green Drake Dun (*Drunella grandis*)

(Practice drawing and coloring the mayfly on the opposite page here.)

Green Drake Nymph (*Drunella grandis*)

(Practice drawing and coloring the mayfly on the opposite page here.)

Pale Evening Dun (*Heptagenia* sp.)

(Practice drawing and coloring the rainbow trout on the opposite page here.)

Rainbow Trout (*Oncorhynchus mykiss*)

www.ingramcontent.com/pod-product-compliance
Lightning Source LLC
Chambersburg PA
CBHW042015110726

48006CB00004B/1096